The Unspoken Symphony

A collection of emotions we all often fail to express

VIVEK SINGH RANA

India | USA | UK

Copyright © VIVEK SINGH RANA
All Rights Reserved.

This book has been self-published with all reasonable efforts taken to make the material error-free by the author. No part of this book shall be used, reproduced in any manner whatsoever without written permission from the author, except in the case of brief quotations embodied in critical articles and reviews.

The Author of this book is solely responsible and liable for its content including but not limited to the views, representations, descriptions, statements, information, opinions, and references ["Content"]. The Content of this book shall not constitute or be construed or deemed to reflect the opinion or expression of the Publisher or Editor. Neither the Publisher nor Editor endorse or approve the Content of this book or guarantee the reliability, accuracy, or completeness of the Content published herein and do not make any representations or warranties of any kind, express or implied, including but not limited to the implied warranties of merchantability, fitness for a particular purpose.

The Publisher and Editor shall not be liable whatsoever...

Made with ❤ on the BookLeaf Publishing Platform
www.bookleafpub.in
www.bookleafpub.com

Dedication

"To the souls navigating life's twists and turns, may these words be a reminder that you are not alone in your thoughts and emotions."

"To my sister, who always supported me and helped me & to my friends who appreciated my writings and encouraged me to write, and have inspired me to share my words with the world."

&

"To my muse जिसने मुझे **Prerna** दी, and sparked my creativity."

Preface

It's 2025, and I am in that stage of life when one is surrounded by chaos, let it be family, friends, academics, relationships, responsibilities, or ambitions. Everything just keeps pulling you apart, forcing one to rethink the choices one has made so far. At this stage, all of us are trying to find peace: a balance, a home. I've never written professionally before, but this is my first effort in that direction. This collection of poetry is a reflection of what I have witnessed and somewhat experienced. The poems are filled with various emotions that probably most of us have experienced and can relate to. As a PhD scholar, I was eager to pen my thoughts and compose some poetry, but was hesitant. I am deeply grateful to my elder sister (Santoshi) and my friends [Bobbin, Rahul, Ruchi, and many more] for their unwavering encouragement, honest feedback, and belief in my voice when I was uncertain.

The protagonist of these poems is not me; everyone who can relate themself to these emotions embedded in these poetry becomes the protagonist. I hope these words resonate with those who find themselves in a similar situation, offering them a voice and a shared space of understanding. May these verses provide comfort, reflection, and a sense of connection, reminding each reader that they are not alone in their experiences and emotions. Through these poems, the personal becomes universal, and every reader is invited to step into the narrative as the central figure of their own story.

Vivek Singh Rana

Acknowledgements

I would like to express my sincere gratitude to **BookLeaf Publishing** for providing this invaluable platform that has enabled me to share my work with a wider audience. Their support and dedication to fostering creative voices have been instrumental in bringing this project to life.

Thank you.

1. Roses

From ancient times, a symbol of love,
A gift from heaven, a gift from above.
A fiery heart, on a thorny stem,
A whispered promise, a lover's gem.
A Red Rose blooms, a timeless art,
The love that's true, the love that's in the heart.

Counting petals for a "yes" or "no"
a dilemma only lovers know.
Plucking each petal, a hopeful fight,
a prayer from the heart, a desire for daylight.
Each one packs many mementos
of love, of happiness, of blessings, and vows.
A happy rose, for the beloved,
her sparkling eyes, getting flooded.
A cheerful heart, a joyful soul,
A Red Rose blooms to make you whole.

As innocent as a child,
my heart wavered as she smiled.

The white rose carries, a fresh new page,
Yearning & churning to break the cage.
Where red once burn in passionate flame,
The white rose calls a gentler name.
Of trust, of truth, of second chance,
Of silent vows, of pure romance.

Red rose whispers, "I love you so," White rose murmurs, "Let it go."

2. Chehra

Ek chehra wo anjana sa,
Jo jana pehchana sa lagne lga.

Dheere se un कदमों se wo nazdeek kuch aane lga,
Jaise ek madhur dhun, koi हौले se gungunane lga.

नज़रे milli un नजरों se, नजरों me नज़ारे reh gae.
Kab ye वक्त guzarta gya, hum wahi ठहरे reh gae.

मुस्कराहट ka woh तिल, woh andaaz-e-bayaan,
Har लम्हा jaise tham sa gaya ho meherbaan.

Faaslon ne phir dhire dhire शब्दों ko chura liya.
Jo jazbaat dil me the unko fir हमने bhi chupa liya.

Dil ke darwaze pe दस्तक, Woh ab karti nahi,
Lekin uski यादों ka saaya, Kabhi मरता nahi.

Wo chehra hai jana pehchana sa,
Jo anjana ab lagta hai.

Jise dekh ke subha hoti thi,
wo bas ख्वाबों me ab dikhta hai.

3. Before U & I become we

Before U & I become we.
We have to become a child,
Like a lamb running around freely,
ignoring all the problems and lies.

Before U & I become we,
We have to become adults,
Weaving our way through troubles,
and learning the bitter truths of life.

Before U & I become we,
We have to become strangers,
Letting our fate guide us to each other,
awaiting the inevitable reunion.

Before U & I become we,
We have to become friends,
As friends, we can be each other's shelter,
keeping each other warm in a raging storm.

Before U & I become we,
We have to become calm,
Like quiet sea shores at dawn,
finding peace in stillness and trust.

Before U & I become we,
We have to become ourselves,
Embarking on a journey of self-discovery,
embracing our emotions & flaws.

Before U & I become we,
We have to become healers,
Mending the wounds we hid from the world,
and soothing the storms inside us.

Before U & I become we,
We have to become home,
Not a place, made of stones and wood,
where love rests without conditions.

Before U & I become we,
We have to become fearless,
Trusting that the other will catch the fall,
while stepping together into the dark.

Before U & I become we,
We have to become skies,

Vast and open, holding endless dreams,
beneath stars that witness our promise.

Before U & I become we,
We have to become silent,
Sitting in the absolute quiet,
needing no words for our hearts to speak.

4. Can I Be a Child Again?

In English, we say "**CAN I BE A CHILD AGAIN**".

But in poetry-

Bring back the days when we don't have to worry about tomorrow,
When we laughed like crazy and forgot all our sorrow.
Where the imagination was warm and mellow,
times when friendship wasn't hollow.

When rain meant dancing, not ruined plans,
and joy was found in holding hands.
When crayons were magic, and stories were real,
and every wound of the heart could heal.

When truth was simple, and love was pure,
and tiny smiles made us feel secure.
Take me back to that innocent lane,
where growing up wasn't tied to pain.

Let me run again through fields of grace,
with an untainted soul and honest face.
Can I be a child again, just for a while,
to live those days of endless smile.

Oh, let me return to those years gone by,
before tears taught me how to cry.
To a world untouched by fear and regret,
where childhood lingers and hope is met.

5. Echoes in the Void

I'm half sick of the World,

Surrounded by bodies, yet no soul
like an ancient mariner at the pole.
The days of the past haunt me down
with the memories of us in the town.

The efforts made were all absurd,

Trying to erase the part of you
waiting for someone who makes me theirs too.
have you dreamt of us with a smile
even though we are apart many miles.

In this era, this result was deserved,

Tried building a home with love and care
in this world full of despair.
is it the timing that I'm getting wrong
or is it our curse so strong?

With every passing day, I'm getting submerged.

A mortal journey full of regrets
the path of which we must forget.

6. एक पंछी

एक पंछी,
जिसका सपना ऊँचे उड़कर,
आसमाँ को छू ले।
खोलकर पर अपने, करनी थी दोस्ती तेज़ हवाओं से,
चाहता था बादलों के पार हो जाना।
बस मंज़िल पे निगाह उसकी
चाहता था बस उसको पाना।

मगर जिन हवाओं के करीब जाने को, थी उसने अपने दिल में दी जगह,
उन्हीं हवाओं ने ऐसा भँवर बनाया कि उलझकर, सब कुछ खो बैठा वहां।
जिन हवाओं को उसने अपना सहारा समझा, वही हवाएँ कातिल बन गईं।
उलझ गया उनकी अनजानी डोर में ऐसे, जैसे कोई पतंग सरे-बाज़ार कट गई।
जो उड़ना चाहते थे किसी की कुर्बत में, या किसी सपने को सच कर दिखाना,
उसी ने उन्हें इस क़दर ज़ख्म दिए कि अब बस है 'मौन' और सब कुछ 'वीराना'।

गिरा वो ऐसे उन ऊँचाइयों से, कि फिर से न अपने पंख फैला सका।
टूट गई उड़ान की हर चाहत उसकी, अब अपने ही सपनों का बोझ था।
ना आसमान का मोह, ना ज़मीन का भय। गुज़रता रहा बस यूं ही समय।

अब उड़ता नहीं, बस आसमान निहार लेता है,
टूट गए हैं ख्वाबों के शीशे उसके।
जिस चाहत ने दी थी उड़ने की हिम्मत,
वही अब हर रात उसे खा जाती है।
यह उड़ने की नहीं,
बस जीने की सज़ा है,
कि आसमाँ पास है,
पर छू नहीं सकता।

कभी वो आज़ाद था,
अब बस सांसें हैं जो उड़ना भूल चुकी हैं।
उसकी चाह ने ही उसके पर छीन लिए,
और वो रह गया...
एक पंछी,
जो उड़ नहीं सकता,
पर अब भी आसमान से मोह नहीं छोड़ता।

7.

"LOVE is the reason to HATE"

8. Not him

We sat beneath the willow tree,
where I told u how much I love thee,
I saw the light in your heart's true glow,
But you talk of him, his easy flow.
You smiled, you listened, and you held my hand,
but in your eyes, he is filled to the brim.
I'm not him.

You say he's the one who makes you feel alive,
while I wait in the shadows for my love to strive.
You said his hands know where to begin,
that touch can make, the silence spin.
I held your heart,
not just your chin,
but your gaze wandered back to him.
No, I am not him.

I know the subtle shift when you recall his name,
my heart burns a little with a flinching flame.
You paint his virtues, bold, brave, benevolent, and bright,

his strength, his wit, his way of winning every fight.
You see a king, a champion, grand and tall,
while I feel small, a shadow on the wall.
He's a hero, I'm the faithful friend,
whose lonely, silent love will never end.
It's a place I can't climb to, nor can I swim,
I am not him.

He sees your body, the curve, the limb,
I see your thoughts, life's acronym.
He devours the moment,
I remember the meanings.
You call his love perfect,
and mine a disfigured limb.
No, I am not him.

My love is like a still, deep, running stream,
a quiet, constant comfort, like a dream.
It seeks the soul, the core, the honest grace,
the gentle beauty time cannot erase.
You praise his fire, his hunger, swift and true,
the passion that he takes, the things he does to you.
I'm just the one who waits on passion's brim,
I am not him.

You choose his thrill over my care,
Leaving me to wonder if you'll ever be aware.

The pain grows like thorns in my quiet chest,
Yet I hold on, though it hurts deep under the skin.
No, I am not him.

9. HEALING

Her- I'm healing,
I don't need anyone right now,
I'm learning to be happy on my own.

Meanwhile, Me- I, too, am trying to heal,
All I need is her right now,
I want to be happy, **"with her"**.

You heal in silence,
with calm in your eyes,
building your peace,
below gentle skies.

With every sunrise,
I wish for your touch,
your laughter glows,
I miss it so much.
My heart blooms in dreams of you near,
soft whispers of love you may someday hear.

If healing means waiting,
for your gentle call,
I'll treasure each ache,
I'll carry it all.
Though your heart wanders where I can't go,
I'll send you my love in wind's soft flow.
Let us be sunlight after the rain,
together dancing out of the pain.

I won't break your boundaries,
nor claim its place,
but if one day your heart does see,
a healing that leads back to me,
then maybe love,
so patient and true,
was always waiting **"Me and You"**.

10. Definition of Love

कभी lga
pyaar ka matlab hai,
jo अच्छा lge, उसे पा लेना,
usse apna बना lena,
jo khubsurat लगे,
use duniya se छुपा lena,
सीने se lga lena.

और phir I realised;
"फूल pasand aa jaye toh usse तोड़ना प्रेम nahi hai"

Pyaar छू lene me nahi,
रोक lene me nahi,
bas देखने me hai
aankho se,
मन se.

Agar तोड़ lu,
toh wo फूल nahi rahega,
agar देखता rahu,

toh pura garden महक uthega.
Tum raho wahi,
खिलती raho apni jagha
mai door मुस्कुराता rahunga
yahi toh sachha प्रेम hai,
aise hi निभाता rahunga.

I don't miss you.
I don't miss you.
I don't miss you.
I don't miss you.
I don't miss you.

I do.

12. I don't miss you.

I don't miss you.
In the mornings when sunlight falls in.
Not in the silence between texting.
Not when songs remind me, what could have been.

I don't miss you
in between my heartbeats,
not when the evening turns cold.
nor the nights, tangled in your sheets.

I don't miss you.
when my laughter feels too light,
nor when coffee tastes too sweet,
not the talk, the warmth, the late nights.

I don't miss you
when the moon forgets to hide,
not when the wind slips through my hair,
the way your fingers once slide.

I don't miss you.
when rain knocks on my window,
not on the days i have been low,
nor the dreams, scattered like fallen leaves.
my peaceful home stolen by thieves.

I don't miss you
your goodbyes, the cold shoulder, my silent cries,
not in the crowd,
nor in the empty hall.
no I don't miss you at all.

I don't miss of you
but sometimes the world does it for me.
A whisper in a crowd, a shadow shaped like thee.
But now, in the silence,
I admit it all,
I miss you more than words
I miss you a lot whole.
I miss you like the moon misses the sun.
waiting for our journey, for us to be one.

13. The One

They will find a reason, a moment, a way.
Those who wish to stay,
When someone wants you in their sky,
they move the clouds, they make time fly.
They'll cross the miles, they'll bridge the space,
for love will guide their fateful chase.
When passions are true, they find their way,
through darkest night or brightest day.

Love is not a lonely call,
nor built on tears that softly fall.
It blooms where equal hands have made
a home that is not for trade.
If you must beg for one to stay,
perhaps their path was not your way.
True care will find a path through rain,
through silence, distance, even pain.

They'll find a way to say your name,
to guard your warmth, to keep the flame.

You'll never ask, you'll never plead,
for love that's yours will meet your need.
For when two hearts are meant to stay,
no storm can steal their bond away.
The right one finds you,
through and through,
and chooses you,
as you choose them too.

Two souls that care will always try,
to build, to bridge, to simplify.
But if you chase through empty air,
and find no answer waiting there,
release the ache, let nature prove
some souls aren't meant for your groove.
The right ones don't need to be found,
they walk beside you, safe and sound.

The ones who stay are those who see,
your worth, your peace, your honesty.

14. Why!

Why is it that my mind is a battleground?
Where self-doubt and fear unbound?
Why do I search for flaws in my own soul?
And overlook the cracks in others' role?
Why do I lie awake at night, questioning my existence,
Wondering if I'm just a fleeting thought, a momentary instance?
Do I truly matter, or am I just a speck of dust?
A temporary blip in the cosmos, soon to be lost?

Why do I doubt the nature of reality,
And wonder if my consciousness is just a fantasy?
Am I just a dream within a dream, a never-ending maze?
Or am I a real being, with a purpose and a phase?
Do I truly have control, or am I just a pawn in the game,
A mere mortal, justifying the ways of god to men.

Maybe it's the human condition, this existential mess,
To question our existence and the nature of our distress.

Perhaps it's the fragility of our mortal soul,
That makes us wonder, and makes our hearts cold.

15. My Only Sin

I praised u a lot
It wasn't my fault,
My only fault is that
I kept you at halt.

With you, with you,
I tied my heart's bond.
O beloved,
I have no idea how to respond.

I gave my all, my flashing spark,
a spark that's still keeping me in the dark.
And though you turned, and walked away,
My soul still whispers what words can't say.
The hope I forged, the soul, the mind,
still endless echoes left behind.

I loved you so, that's my only sin.
My only sin, You never knew within.
I wished for you, yet it's no crime,

My heart was true, beyond all time.
But if I blundered, then let it be
The fault is mine, you couldn't see.

With you, with you,
I knew a peace I'll never find.
O beloved,
A treasure left far behind.

For though we part, the passion stays,
Through all the coming nights and days.
My only wish, though now denied,
Was that you'd stay right by my side.
So when you feel the morning dew,
know that my heart is still with you.

I loved you so, for what else could I do?
What could I do, other than loving you.
Though seasons turn and rivers flow,
My heart, it yearns, it won't let go.
But if the cost was my despair,
It was a price I chose to bear

With you, with you,
The world was bright.
O beloved,
Now swallowed by an endless night.

For though we part, our truth remains,
what remains is a song in love's domain.
A love pure, though left undone,
It burned as bright as a thousand suns.
So if I fade, and time moves on,
Remember me when night meets dawn.

I loved you so, and that's our fight.
That's our fight that steals my light.
I prayed for you, that's not a lie,
My love for you will never die.
But if I failed, then let it be,
The blame is mine, for loving thee.

16. You and I

You & I
We are like the pages of a book.
But you are the chapter filled with grace,
And I, the one left blank, a lonely space.

You & I
We are like the echoes of the past.
But you are the memory that will last,
And I, the moment that fades so fast.

You & I
We are like the paths that diverge in the woods.
But you are the trail that's clear, the one that's good,
And I, the one that's lost, the one that's misunderstood.

You & I
We are like the words that are put to the page.
But you are the poem, soothing every age,
And I, the shattered verse that fails to engage.

You & I
We are like the last goodbye, the final farewell.
But you are the memory that stays, the bond one can rekindle,
And I, the moment that's gone, with the sound of the mourning bell.

You & I
We are like the stories left untold.
But you are the chapter that's complete, one that's worth more than gold,
And I, the page that's torn, the one that's left to grow old.

You & I
We are like the stars that we wish upon.
But you are the twinkle that's bright, the sparkle that's won,
And I, the star that's dim, the light that's lost in the dawn.

You & I
We are like the characters in a play.
But you are the story's soul, the reason we watch and pray,
And I, just a prop fixed in the field of hay, only there for display.

You & I

We are like mirrors reflecting the light.
But you are a symbol of objectivity, of self, of truth,
And I, the shattered surface, a broken youth.

You & I

We collide like stars in a midnight sky,
But, I am the proof of love that is ETERNAL.
And you are not even REAL!

17. Me and You

Me and you
We are like memories and the pain.
But I'm the recollection that heals, the memories that remain,
And you're the agony that hurts, the sorrow that forever sustains.

Me & you
We are like the hope and the despair.
But I'm the optimism that lifts, the promise that's always there,
And you're the pessimism that weighs, the doubt that's hard to share.

Me & You
We are like the dreams and the nightmares.
But I'm the vision that's clear, the future that's bright and fair,
And you're the illusion that's dark, the fantasy that's hard to bear.

Me & you
We are like the arms that we share.
But I extend my hands to aid and to care,
And yours are the very hands that ripped my heart open for everyone to stare.

Me and You
We are like the fire and the rain.
But I'm the warmth that soothes and heals the pain,
And you're the storm that chills, the chaos that leaves its stain.

Me and You
We are like the wings and the cage.
But I'm the flight of promise, the freedom on every page,
And you're the bars that bind, the prison built from rage.

Me & you
We are like the mirror and the mask.
But I'm the reflection that's true,
And you're the facade that fools.

Me and You
We are like the endings and the beginnings.
But I'm the hope, the newness in a wounded heart,

And you're the closure that everyone finds as they depart.

18.

Just remember,
I'm Here For You

19. The Prisoner

She whispers words, so sweet and kind,
But echoes of the past, I find.
A broken trust, a shattered vow,
A fear that haunts her, even now.
Her love, so warm and so bright,
Yet shadows dance, consuming light.

She pushes me back, with words so cold,
A fortress built, a story un-told.
She hurts me now, to save herself,
A prisoner I'm, of her wounded self.
I know the pain, the silent cry,
And offer hope, beneath the sky.

I wait for her, an unfinished statue,
hoping someday she will see me through.
The journey's long, the path unclear,
But in her eyes, I find a love sincere.
I'm waiting for her to break the chain,
And let me in, to ease the pain.

Together now, with open eyes,
We greet the sun, mesmerized.
No ghosts remain, no looming fear,
Just you and me drawn near.
Hand in hand, our sorrows past,
We build a bond that's meant to last.

20. The Logic of the Heart

Ten souls stand on the shore,
watching.
Nine would dive,
arms open, calling your name
with soft tides of patience.
But you,
You walked past their warmth,
eyes fixed on the **One,**
who wouldn't even let the waves
touch their feet.

This is how hearts work
they chase the cold,
forgetting the ones who offer fire.
We crave what turns away,
we love what won't stay,
and call the hurt a kind of fate.

It's strange
how the same heart that beats for love

breaks because of it, too.
This is the bitter, broken logic of heart,
to trade a mountain of comfort
for a single, slippery slope.

The nine are now a distant shore,
And you are sinking
choking on the very water,
nine others would have swum through,
just to hold your head above the waves.
You drown, not in a storm,
but in the silence of the one who chose to stay dry.

You spend your strength,
not toward the shore,
but towards their gaze,
a gaze that is not even on you.

We row
our fragile boats of hope
onto the rough and reckless tide,
past the calm ports, straight toward the storm.
Why?
Because the chase feels like
the proof of feeling,
and the sharp pain
is mistaken as a sign of being alive.

It is a troublesome, terrible truth we carry
that the deepest desire to be loved is the very
thing that breaks us apart.
Like that relentless, lonely sea,
which is an immortal art.

21. Unwritten Paths

Might our destiny have changed,
had we crossed paths before,
Before the world painted your untainted heart,
into an endless mosaic,
a mosaic etched with anguish & grief!

Perhaps I could have caught the shards
before they carved their fears deep,
or whispered the songs of solace
to the shadows where you sleep.
Maybe I could have been the light that,
guided you through the darkest night,
or the calm within the storm
that raged with all its might.

My heart bleeds for what could've been,
for the love that we might've known.
For the laughter, the adventures,
the memories that could've been our own.
Let us hold on to hope, my love,

and never let it fade,

For I know that together,
We can rise above the pain and the shade.
We can create a new mosaic,
one that's etched with love and light,
A masterpiece that shines so brightly,
that it guides us through the darkest night.

Perhaps the path was meant to twist,
to lead us here, at last,
where we embrace the present,
and let go of the past.

22. Reflections for the Self

Is it a memory that you see,
Or a dream that guides thee?

Do you dare to weave a future, full of hope and might,
Or find refuge in the lost memory's gentle light?

Are you chasing shadows of what remains,
Or painting tomorrows with colours that will forever sustain?

Do you dwell in moments forever gone,
Or shape the promise of a dawn yet unknown?

Do u feel scared that dreams might not come true,
Or brave enough to remember the hands that held you through?

Do you sing the songs of yesteryear's fading tune,
Or compose a symphony beneath the rising moon?

Do you hold close the echoes of laughter once shared,
While knowing some journeys can never be repaired?

Do you mourn the chapters that were closed and done,
Or celebrate the journey that has just begun?

So dream, though dreams may falter and flee,
For memory and hope both set the spirit free.

23.

"Dream it, chase it, make the stars align,
Take your whole life, and write it into a rhyme."

24. Choices Made, Paths Embraced

When the foot steps out, a decision made,
Let the dust of the past softly fade.
Once you choose to move on,
The past is behind,
Let no looking backward confuse your mind.

When you offer your faith to a friend's honest gaze,
Let go of your worries throughout the days.
Once you choose to trust,
Let suspicion release,
Embrace the conviction and find inner peace.

When a worthy new goal is the prize to obtain,
Pour all of your energy, despite any pain.
Once you choose to try,
Don't give up at any cost,
Give everything you have, or the battle is lost.

When a passion is found that you hold so dear,

Let the feelings be perfect, let it be clear.
Once you choose to love,
Then let nothing depart,
But love without limits and all of your heart.

When you pledge your intention to others around,
Let your word be as solid as a rock on the ground.
Once a promise is made,
Your honour's at stake,
Keep it unbroken, for integrity's sake.

Stand firm in the wake of the choices you keep,
And you shall sow the harvest where others just weep.

25. The Journey

I live through life with laughter and tears,
No longer held back by doubts and fears.
My journey is long, and far from over,
and I'm afraid I don't carry a four-leaf clover.
Lost many battles, and duels, and jewels,
my precious companions turned into ghouls.
A friend was molded by those warm hands that once carried
the weight of trust, now shattered and buried.

Stories we pen in the Book of Life,
chapters I can't summarise even in the afterlife.
Tales that are yet to be, carrying happiness and joy,
an aspiring journey, where dreams will deploy.
With every stumble, I rise and mend,
Each fall, a lesson, each scar a friend.

The winds may howl, the storms may roar,
But I am the captain who'll reach the shore.
So I'll live through life with courage and grace,

Welcoming challenges I'm destined to face.
The path ahead, though unknown, I'll embrace,
For it's there that I'll find my place.

26. Shades of Love

One man's toy
is another man's princess.
One man's burden
is another man's blessing.
One man's nightmare
is another's sweet dream.
One man's chaos
is another man's peace.
One man's "too much"
is another's everything,
One man's regret
is another man's prize.
One sees her flaws
where another considers art.

One man's fleeting phase is another man's start,
Of a forever that beats in his heart.

27.

"I'm so glad u came into the world,
and I'm more than glad that you came into my world."

"Happy Birthday"

:)

28. 28 November

The day when the universe sealed our fate,
It was near the end of November, a precious date.
A cry was heard echoing in the room
completing the family, making it bloom.
A little baby girl, tiny limbs curled tight,
Her first breath whispered hope into the night.

Years passed, threads crossed, fortune spun,
until my days tangled quietly with yours, undone.
It was our fate and our stars, uniting beneath the starlit dome,
I found my journey's purpose, found my home.
So here is my song, I'll forever remember,
for the soul who was born on the 28th of November.

Your short height reaches softly up to my chest,
and your petite hand in mine quietly blessed.
Your hair, so dark and long and thick,
left on my pillow when the morning clock ticks.
Your short-tempered attitude keeps me at bay,

but I still wanna be with you night and day.

Through years of wandering, I found my way to you,
Drawn by the pull of a love ever true.
Oh, my love, born on that November night,
You are the fate that made my darkness bright.
And in your story, I find my own reign,
A love eternal, through joy and through pain :)

29.

Her trembling heart, behind the door,
Still fears the hurt it felt before.
I do not rush, I do not plead,
For time will grow the tender seed.

And if the world is too cruel to you,
Remember, I'll always be there for you.

30. Reasons Why I Can't Be Just Friends With You

Reasons Why I Can't Be Just Friends With You-

1- I tell myself to stay your friend, but my heart never listens to me,
It aches when you talk about someone else; it stings like a bee.

2 - I borrow your words, wear them all day,
At least in language we are one, as they say.

3 - I know what you love, every song, every place, every food, every thread,
Yet I also know that I'm not among the things you said.

4 - You're so much more than a person, deep like the sea,
A feeling that refuses to fade, woven deep inside of me.

5 - I remember too much: your dress that day,
the place we first met, how we found our way,
The shade of brown that lives in your eyes,
Your long, thick hair's swirling beneath morning skies.
The meals that u cooked and served me like a queen,
the nights we spent unraveling haunted scenes.

6 - I've cherished you too fondly, treasured each sign and clue,
To settle for friendship when my soul yearns for more with you.

31. When You are Mine

Life is but a fleeting moment, you see,
This bond we share, centuries aren't enough for me.
So I'll ask the heavens for a little more time,
This is where I want to be, and it's worth every dime.
If you are my peace, my heart's true friend,
Every pain feels beautiful, with you it can mend.

Your smiles are my strength, my guiding light,
In them, I find hope shining so bright.
Though the world may bring its trials and strife,
In your embrace, I find the essence of life.
Life has become a canvas, painted so fine,
What more could heaven offer when you are mine?

32.

It feels like yesterday we were laughing till three,
Now, I'm left wondering. Do you even think of me?

33. बेखबर वो, बैचैन मैं

Wo कहती hai abhi time nahi,
Par friends ke saath chali jaati hai sheher.
Mere intzaar ko wo jaane na jaane,
Main adhoori raat ka tanha safar.

Kab tak rahu main यूं tanha,
Tere khayalon ka sahara liye,
Hasi ke wo pal yaad aate hain,
Jo tere sath guzare hue.

Uske schedule me naam nahi mera,
Par main ab bhi likhta uska liye ye jazbaat,
Wo friends ke saath coffee pe nikle,
Aur main intezaar karu har ek raat.

Kabhi poocha tha usne, kya hua?
Aaj wo bhi sawal kahin kho gaye.
Main ab bhi wahi chhod aaya hoon khud ko,
Jahan hum dono pehle रो gaye.

Phone uske haath se छुटता nahi,
Par mere message ka jawab der se aata.
Dusron ke status pe haste hue emoji,
Mera khayal aaye to sirf ek "hann" bheja jata.

Milte hain jab toh नज़रे chura leti hai,
Baat karu to bas sir hila deti hai.
Jo kal tak thi hasin muskurahat sirf mere liye,
Aaj wahi muskurahat sabke dikha deti hai.

Wo kehti hai busy ho ab main,
Har baar yehi baat कही jaaye.
Main baitha hoon tere intezaar mein,
Tu toh kisi aur mein kho jaaye.

Mujhe lagta hoon main अजनबी,
Aur wo sabke liye sab kuch ban gayi.
Phir bhi dil kehta, ruk ja abhi,
Abhi na ja, main hoon यहीं.

34. End !

The End is near, a mystery unknown,
Lurking in shadows, it's never shown.
It surprises us, with a sudden might,
Leaving us breathless, in the dark of night,
It's a shock, a moment of awe and fear,
a reminder of how fragile we are here.
A whisper so silent, yet heavy with fate,
Time marches forward; it never will wait.
We try to hold on, but it slips away fast,
The end is a reminder to cherish the past.
It's a lesson in living, in loving and letting go,
A chance to find closure and a new path to know.

www.ingramcontent.com/pod-product-compliance
Lightning Source LLC
Chambersburg PA
CBHW060350050426
42449CB00011B/2915